Praise for **Scrape the Velv**

M000118196

"*Scrape the Velvet from Your Antlers* travels wondro
city streets to find what matters: the gorgeous love, the all-consuming desire, the joy of
human touch. This collection sings, pounds, and shouts. McQuain's keen eye and sharp
words command us to stop and see. *Scrape the Velvet* is a treat of a book, rendered by a man
at the peak of his craft."
    —**Jonathan Corcoran**, author of *The Rope Swing*

"In *Scrape the Velvet from Your Antlers*, maturity is shown as a toughening process, a paring
away of uncertainty. In the West Virginia of his childhood, McQuain finds himself a young
gay man struggling against an alien and discriminatory culture. In elegant poems, so much
of a place and time, he goes from the boy eager to please an exacting father intent on
building a house, to the Good Samaritan in the big city where he has landed, stopping in
traffic to talk a would-be suicide down from a bridge. In lyrical lines that stretch out where
they need to, never losing momentum, he blends a Keatsian sweetness with the street smarts
of a Frank O'Hara. 'As you take the hill, the hill takes you.' It is 'stubbled with stubborn
flowers,' the deer he views, 'a blister / of orange-red and velvet need.' And in the lush final
poem, the simple feast of Italian ices from a South Philly vendor that the poet shares in bed
with his lover one hot summer night he rightly names 'this moment / a victory.'"
    —**Elaine Terranvova**, author of *The Diamond Cutter's Daughter: a Poet's Memoir*

"[H]ow easily the things we do go awry— / what can we // expect of truth / when we don't
dig for proof / or plumb its depth?" And digging for truth is what Kelly McQuain does in
poem after beautiful poem in his moving collection *Scrape the Velvet from Your Antlers*. The
speaker in this book knows deeply the language of rural landscape and lives in the space
where landscape and body merge. McQuain also understands grief and leaving, following
the "[s]omething [that] calls you somewhere else." These are generous poems, ravenous to
love a broken world. Whether McQuain's speaker is at a circuit party or trying to talk down
a man who wants to jump from a bridge, there is a through line of tenderness, a lived-in
melancholy. His longing becomes our longing."
    —**Aaron Smith**, author of *The Book of Daniel*

"McQuain's poems stun with tenderness and revelation. The poet sings of burlap and
cornsilk, wolves and drag-queens, and the heart shuddering like unripe fruit against Dolly's
billowy chest as he confronts the accumulation and loss of this life while searching for a
soft place to land."
    —**Sonja Livingston**, author of *Ghostbread*

"Kelly McQuain has written a book of poems both poignant and mesmerizing. The
complexities of family relationships are examined here with a no-holds-barred frankness
that makes it impossible not to recall the nearly overwhelming power of emotional
dissonance in our own early lives. There is also an intricate look at how a burgeoning
sexuality can further complicate entry into the world as we know it. However, the texture
of these poems is wonderfully rich; McQuain's poems have a cinematic quality that is hard
to resist. I quickly found myself caught in the current of *Scrape The Velvet from Your Antlers*,
feeling compelled to read just one more poem and then another and then just one more."
    —**Tim Seibles**, author of *One Turn Around the Sun*

Scrape
the
Velvet
from
Your Antlers

The TRP Southern Poetry Breakthrough Series
Series Editor: J. Bruce Fuller

The TRP Southern Poetry Breakthrough Series highlights a debut full-length collection by emerging authors from each state in the southern United States.

Books in this Series:

Scrape the Velvet from Your Antlers

poems

Kelly McQuain

The TRP Southern Poetry Breakthrough Series: West Virginia

TRP: The University Press of SHSU

Library of Congress Cataloging-in-Publication Data
Names: McQuain, Kelly, author.
Title: Scrape the velvet from your antlers : poems / Kelly McQuain.
Other titles: TRP Southern poetry breakthrough series.
Description: First edition. | Huntsville, Texas : TRP: The University Press
  of SHSU, [2023] | Series: The TRP Southern poetry breakthrough series:
  West Virginia
Identifiers: LCCN 2022038481 (print) | LCCN 2022038482 (ebook) | ISBN
  9781680033328 (paperback) | ISBN 9781680033335 (ebook)
Subjects: LCSH: West Virginia—Poetry. | LCGFT: Poetry. | Gay poetry.
Classification: LCC PS3613.C587474 S37 2023 (print) | LCC PS3613.C587474
  (ebook) | DDC 811/.6—dc23/eng/20220822
LC record available at https://lccn.loc.gov/2022038481
LC ebook record available at https://lccn.loc.gov/2022038482

FIRST EDITION

Cover design by Bradley Alan Ivey
Cover Image: Painting by Kelly McQuain

Printed and bound in the United States of America
First Edition Copyright ©2023

Published by TRP: The University Press of SHSU
Huntsville, Texas 77341
texasreviewpress.org

TABLE OF CONTENTS

Introduction

by Jeff Mann

I've been teaching at Virginia Tech since 1989, and, as university professors go, I'm fairly unconventional, or so my students tell me. My pickup truck, my love for country music, my myriad tattoos, my Appalachian accent, and my voluminous Viking-style salt-and-pepper beard all seem to defy their expectations of what an academic and a gay man should look like.

Another trait of mine my students find surprising but often share is my passionate love for DC and Marvel movies. Such fare many snooty academics would regard with supercilious contempt as an audiovisual version of "genre fiction," in particular speculative fiction, which is to say science fiction and fantasy. Luckily, I'm well past the age when I might have cared what my fellow professors think about much of anything, and my enthusiasm for such popular entertainments as *Wonder Woman, Thor,* and *The Avengers* encourages my students to regard me as more approachable, less aloof Ivory-Tower intellectual.

And what has all this to do with Kelly McQuain's vivid, lucid, and musical poetry collection, *Scrape the Velvet from Your Antlers*?

For decades, time travel has been a popular trope in speculative fiction, a vivid contemporary example being *Avengers: Endgame* (2019). As I read McQuain's book, I kept wishing that I could go back in time to give the book to a younger version of myself, the Jeff Mann of 1976-77. That shaggy-haired mountain boy enamored of dark beards, hard biceps, and hairy chests would have benefited greatly from this collection's wonderful mix of gay and Appalachian elements.

Like McQuain, I grew up in West Virginia—he in Randolph County and I in Summers County. Like McQuain, I realized in my adolescence that I was attracted to men. Coming to terms with one's gay identity is often difficult to begin with. Coming to terms with such an identity in rural Appalachia can be especially fraught, thanks to the ubiquity of fundamentalist Christianity (effectively depicted in McQuain's "Mercy") and the rarity of gay representation and role models. Such a deep sense of difference, mentioned in the title poem, and the perceived need to keep such difference a secret, can be profoundly alienating. "Difference burned too—I knew the sting of its blisters," says McQuain in "Southern Heat."

Ex nihilo, the title of the first section of this collection, is apropos: gay youth sometimes have to create an identity out of next to nothing. "What if you never meet / the person you are meant to be?" McQuain asks in "Scrape the Velvet from Your Antlers." I was lucky: I met some version of that person in high school. My tenth-grade biology teacher, Jo Davison, came out to me as a lesbian, as did two friends, "Bill" and Brenda. When Jo introduced me to the novels of Patricia Nell Warren—*The Front Runner* (1974) and *The Fancy Dancer* (1976)—they became the first of a long series of books that helped me come to terms with my same-sex attractions.

Difference often creates an uncomfortable sense of displacement, as McQuain makes clear: "But where to learn / of this authentic self? / Not on this hill, not in that house. / Something calls you somewhere else." Like many rural-raised gays and lesbians, I can well relate. I left my small town as quickly as I could, in search of better romantic and erotic opportunities in that "somewhere else." I attended West Virginia University for both undergraduate and graduate school, swilling years of beer in Morgantown's rotating series of gay bars, even as the AIDS crisis loomed, that "ravenous age of plague," that "petal cage of desire and death." How adeptly McQuain captures those years, "the grand movie of being young," in poems like "Monkey Orchid" and "Rain in Old Movies."

"Somewhere else" for McQuain ended up being Philadelphia, where he's flourished for many years. Included in this volume are several fine poems depicting that city, among them "Lent," "Nobody's Savior," "Two Girls in West Philly Spray Their Hair into Beehives," and "Tonight Guanyin Seeks an End to Suffering." I, on the other hand, got as far as the Maryland suburbs of Washington DC, spent one homesick semester there, then returned to the mountains, having realized that city living was not for me. What a surprising revelation: my native region, the Appalachian South, which I had once been so eager to escape, was, ironically, where I belonged. There was no denying my heritage, my roots.

McQuain may reside in Philadelphia, but the mountain roots he and I share are more than evident in this brilliant collection. Reading these poems, I often think of Loyal Jones' seminal text, "Appalachian Values," in which he lists typical traits of mountain-born folks: Religion; Independence, Self-Reliance and Pride; Neighborliness; Familism; Personalism; Love of Place; Modesty; Sense of Beauty; Sense of Humor; and Patriotism.

The first, "Religion," I've mentioned above—Appalachia's many brands of judgmental and intolerant Christianity—and McQuain makes it clear that being "locked in that furnace boiler of church and youth" creates guilt, confusion, and internal turmoil. "All hellfire, all brimstone," he says of his racist step-grandfather in "Southern Heat."

"Appalachian people are family centered," Loyal Jones claims in the "Familism" section, and McQuain's poetry illustrates that quality profusely.

The poems about his parents and siblings, among them "My Father's Shop," "Architect," "Creation Myth," "No Trespassing," Uncle," "Siege Engine," and "The Grieving Bone" are some of the most haunting and poignant poems in this collection.

"Love of Place" is evident in McQuain's rich use of natural detail, describing the landscapes in which he was raised: "Summer and the pureness of a wooded hillside," "the dew still collects, and the insects and crickets blur to song." Here are "the day's hot ricochet of blue bottle flies/ and bees gone crazy in their looping," here are "Joe-Pye weed and yarrow root," "a line of pines / gloating their evergreen promise of shade." Lines like these take me back to my own country childhood and remind me of how deeply I've learned to love the terrain and biodiversity of the Southern Appalachians.

"Love of Place" intertwines with "Sense of Beauty," I think. Years ago, I wrote a book about where I find beauty, *Loving Mountains, Loving Men*. Not surprisingly, McQuain seems to find beauty in the same places as I. The love poems in this volume are deft and melodic, paeans of praise and thanks for the beauty of men, the beauty of men's bodies together—"Two hims"—and the lives that two men can share. "Tongue," "Constellation," "Thirst," "Two Hymns," and "Strawberries, Limoncello, Water Ice, Passing Time" are among my favorites.

Finally, my younger self would be happy to learn McQuain is a superhero fan, too, with references to "little Kal-El in his speedy rocket" as well as the demonic Vampirella, who serves as both a muse and a symbol of rebellion for McQuain back in his comic-collecting childhood.

No time travel. Teenage Jeff would have loved this book, but he was denied it. Middle-age Jeff, on the other hand, has enjoyed it immensely and related to it powerfully. Thanks to Kelly McQuain! It's a real privilege to help usher this superb book into the world.

Scrape
the
Velvet
from
Your Antlers

For John

and for my family—

those born of blood
and those we choose.

i:
ex nihilo

Camping as Boys in the Cow Field

Summer and the pureness of a wooded hillside,
the far dark of evening come to meet our fire smoke
on the old farm, our tent up and the cows away,
rabbits in the grass as the first slow sweep
of the light tower above the little landing strip comes to life.
Feel the vibration of the cows and how even now
the dew still collects, and the insects and crickets blur to song.
Our minds were the sky and the sky was our minds;
what we knew of brotherhood was shared not with brothers
          but friends.
Our legs shook as we climbed the tower,
hand then foot, rung after rung, minds drunk with dizziness
as our eyes translated the stars from dots of light to wonder.
As the light circled, we stumbled upon a first high
and let go of our solid selves, hearts radiant and red
as stamped tin trinkets in some future Mexico.
Later there would be cheap wine and girls,
the light of those nights diffuse by now and a part
of all space. Did we know then how everything in the world
is connected, like the wounds of Christ eternally exposed?
And you with a finger in the wound. And you with salt.

Scrape the Velvet from Your Antlers

As you take the hill, the hill takes you—
raking you and your siblings into
a grassy sway of beetles and spiders moving,
and the day's hot ricochet of blue bottle flies
and bees gone crazy in their looping.
Your brother and sister run to catch the horizon.
You wade slowly through the lashing,
alive with combustion, eager for bursting.
This hill, once a forest, has long been cut low,
untilled, rock-strewn, stubbled
with stubborn flowers. Soapwort,
Queen Anne's lace, whorled loosestrife
seeded scattershot, while—downhill—

laundry bows a slender line and inside a house
men tune fiddles, a banjo strums—
melody in the making. But you have no time
for the old-timiness of old men, won't be quaintly
clothespinned. You are Joe-Pye weed and yarrow root,
resolute with purpose, pinioned for sky.
Why then is your skin nothing but cockleburs?
Who fiddled with you—rewired *deference*
into *difference*? What if you never meet
the person you are meant to be? The future
is a cocked gun—pretty, but peacock mean—

and you are devil's paintbrush,
a blister of orange-red and velvet need.
You've yet to steady into friends
who will ride life's curves with you,
yet to meet men come to wreck you.
There is only the splintered heart of now:
this house, this hill—a horizon spurned
as you cast your gaze down-road, past trailers,
to a line of pines
gloating their evergreen promise of shade.
What kneels to drink in that dark?
What hooved thing—some player
of panpipes moving? A preacher
might call this moment choosing.

Only nine
and already you've packed up your belonging
—every out-of-bound path
boyhood's sweet undoing.
This hill beneath your feet is cracked,
as aching as an insect's rasp. When a tune
ignites from the house you feel its lull,
its *not quite yet*. Imagine a table
where comfort food lies spread.
But what if you'd rather be the hunger
than a child spoon-fed?
A lick of wind on nape of neck,
a secret transmission that coils and threads
as grasshoppers leap away like longing.
Someday soon you'll understand

how music marks a mating move,
how forewing against notched leg strums
the same tune teenage boys knead
into the pockets of fraying jeans
as they bum for smokes and try their luck
among trucks purring in parking lots.
Their plea? *Unravel me,*
snap me free of all ties. Show me answers
apart from lies. But where to learn
of this authentic self?
Not on this hill, not in that house.
Something calls you somewhere else.

Brave

From rough burlap we cut loincloths, fringed the ends,
strung cheap plastic beads into wampum belts,
sucking our thumbs when our needles drew blood
—done not so much for merit badges as for
the Kool-Aid crazed shenanigans got up to that day
in our frazzled den mother's cluttered house:
ersatz "Indian" finery pulled over blue uniforms
as we danced and whooped and bounced
from LaZ-Boy recliner to afghan-covered couch.
A turkey feather fell from my paper headband
on the long walk home through kickable leaves.
Part of a pack, but where was my true tribe?
Those happy Cubs? Boys whose hands
I sometimes longed to hold, hard like a toy tomahawk.
I needed stealth, a new way to hide in the world:
patient as stone, elusive as water. I wanted to become
a stranger to myself, someone stronger in different skin.
I knew my bedroom slippers were not moccasins
that night as I stood naked before my closet mirror—
lipstick warpaint striping my cheeks, a welcome scratch
of burlap on my hairless balls (it was always
so *involved* being me). No uniform. No fear. No one to see.
I was alone and for once loving my aloneness. My body
an arrow shooting somewhere far off, its bow and quiver
triggered in this act of making the invisible visible at last.
Fringe on my loincloth tickled my thighs and knees
as I wound my wampum belt around my waist
and wondered what my new name should be:
Feathered Dream-Catcher? (we had one in the kitchen)
Or *He Who Sees Shapes in the Random Patternicity of Things*?
But I was only a kid too quiet in his room;
at the sound of someone's feet on the stairs, I hid.
A turn of the doorknob and my father leaned in to ask
what the hell was I doing crawling under the bed?
He laughed as I rose, my hands hiding my bare chest,
my pale skin reddening as I stammered to explain.
I couldn't explain. What was I in his eyes? A silly boy,
his little wild thing. So I laughed, too—what else could I do
as I stood before him revealed: being scared, being brave.

My Father's Shop

Any snips and snails that may have
once made him had gotten lost in years
of elbow grease and oil changes: life

in the antique shop where my father painted
business signs in back, where cherry bombs
and peanut snacks circled on a dusty rack

when my little-boy hands reached to take them.
We lived upstairs above that roadside shop,
full of my father's endless accumulating

junk: rusty toy trucks, heavy oak furniture,
faded *Playboys* from the early 1960s.
Nothing ever seemed to sell. Clutter rules

your life when the whole world's collectible:
old postcards and photographs, kewpie dolls,
yellowing maps—vintage ephemera

already working to invent me into an adult
easily enchanted and defeated by nostalgia.
There too, in his shop, stood the naked fact

he and I never talked of sports, or how to bait
a fishing hook. In silence I watched him paint,
stenciling letter after letter as my own fingers traced

heroes and sidekicks in dog-eared comic books—
working my way through accumulation and loss
the way my mother, upstairs in a room

sewing patches on jeans, darning our socks,
might work a needle slowly
                            through worn-out cloth.

Dolly

At ten even this boy wanted to have them:
what older girls in training bras
had taken to padding we manufactured
with balloons swelling our t-shirts
as we sang, my younger sister & I,
to Dolly Parton on the car radio, the slosh
of automated car-wash rollers slapping
against roof & window, & Daddy
for once not yelling at our backseat
performance. I was falling in love
with Dolly, that hillbilly Valkyrie,
her platinum hair-do a spun-sugar miracle,
her hummingbird voice a God-given weapon
against heartache, life's missed takes,
hardscrabble lessons about getting
the things we weren't getting but wanted—
Dolly, the doll I could never have,
her songs hungry & angry & funny—
a golden-throated spiritual connection
to the busty Daisy Mae hidden inside me.
My Dolly-pops squeaked as I rubbed
their knotted nipples, the car wash's
soapy water and brushes almost through,
& Dolly still singing "Here You Come Again"
as Daddy strummed the steering wheel
and lit a cigarette, while Dolly offered
a quick wink, all glitter & glue,
with eyes that could tell if a man
was a happy drunk, a sad or mad one—
& me, a balloon-breasted boy still singing
for a tender bosom to lay his head upon.

Vampirella

It wasn't her boobs that appealed to this gay fellow
or the fact that she wore a red bikini thong.
She was a superhero with fangs, my gal Vampirella

—no tangled-up Rapunzel, no ashen Cinderella.
An ass-kicker in knee boots ready to get it on
with any handsome, hot-blooded earthly fellow.

I fell under her spell too, I have to tell you,
though her curves didn't appeal to my ten-year-old dong.
Still I was bewitched and bedeviled by Vampirella

and her pulp-mag adventures, their pages long yellowed
along with old comics left in boxes too long.
In back of the Book Mart, past the fat owner fella,

is where I found her, a slick cover by Frazetta
peeking out past *Creepy* and *Eerie*, one shelf-rung
below forbidden *Playboy*: my wild bitch, *Vampirella!*

She fought werewolves, demons, witches, night terrors;
she seduced handsome men with her succubus song.
Though I followed her stories, I never could tell

a soul that I wanted what every straight fellow shouldn't:
to be a hot vampire chick and super-strong—
my high-heeled, raven-haired, bikini-clad Vampirella.

At ten, I was a good kid, no holy terror,
though I suspect my parents feared I was turning out wrong.
Maybe that's why they let their queer little fellow

spend his allowance on soft-core mags that might quell
a desire already starting to steer him along.
Blame me. Don't you dare blame double-D Vampirella.

Architect

My father's name for me was shit-for-brains
those long days we spent clearing the hillside of brush.
The whine of his chainsaw in the late-autumn cold,
my arms numb from stacking wood in the truck.
I was distracted, never moved quick enough,
wishing the day would fall aside like dead leaves,
eager to return home come dusk.
To a home that wasn't a home, not really,
but another of my father's make-do inventions:
a cinderblock building he built for his auction business
but moved us into
when he lost the house we rented.

Sign painter, antiques dealer, real estate salesman, auctioneer.
And now, an architect.
My father's old self-hoods constantly
sputtered into embers.
I was less a son than a reluctant assistant
to a poor-man magician
robbing Peter to pay Paul for each new venture.
I learned lessons in painting and polishing junk;
I made the honor roll in teenage resentment.   I learned
what I did and didn't want to become:
slapped together
like the walls of our little apartment,
chipboard thin when I wanted to keep everyone out—
picture a different kind of life.
In my bedroom, there wasn't even a window.

But then my father bought this little half-cleared lot
up a winding, dirt-road holler:
the old family farm,   sold off piecemeal by an uncle.
The promise now of our first good family home,
an overdue correction,
but couldn't Dad see I'd be off at college
before the foundation he poured cemented?

I watched him stay up late over stubborn blueprints,
told him river-rock siding was a good idea
but windows needed to open.
It took years, but he laid the gas and water lines himself,

managed the house's framing and the laying of its roof.
Then cancer: a lifetime of smoking
and cleaning paint from his hands with turpentine-soaked rags.
He died in the "temporary" cinderblock apartment,
                    left the world with work undone.

My father, the architect, drew impossible blueprints
          this shit-for-brains somehow finds a way to follow:
All the things I want to finish but don't,
                    they keep me up these late-night hours.
I'm still clearing brush out of my head up that hollow,
          chainsaw-teeth biting into soft pulp.
I want leaves and branches
     to rise back to their trees, but time won't reverse
                              —it only devours.
My father stands in the failing light, yells at me to hurry up.

Southern Heat

It was my step-grandfather who said the Word
as we drove through a blur of Georgia peanut fields
past black kids sitting on shanty stoops:
a boy and girl not much older than me—
cornrow hair, dirt on their feet. And though
I'd never heard the Word
before that family visit south,
I knew what it meant the moment
my grandfather opened his mouth. Hot wind
through the window wouldn't blow it away.
My fault? I was the one who'd made him say
the Word when I pointed out the window
to ask *Who're they?*

I couldn't offer the awkward chuckle
someone else in the car did—my mother?
older brother? I knew their hiccup of laughter hid
the same disappointment I felt in this man.
He didn't understand: *words hurt.* I did.
At seven, I already knew "faggot", I knew "queer".
I knew my step-grandfather, studying to be a preacher,
had his own messed-up cross to bear
having lost his first wife and six kids nine years before
in a house fire while he was out working
the railroad graveyard shift.
Difference burned, too —I knew the sting of its blisters—
yet hot Georgia dust clawed at my throat
as my granddad's car tore down that gravel road.
Houses and fields swept by. Light whipped
like a cotton sheet. I sat down, the hot vinyl seat
burning me. I was burning alive!
Damn if I didn't hate everyone
the way I hated myself inside.

Our gas was low so we stopped
at an old clapboard store to pee and fill up.
While Grandpop stood working the pump
my brother and I followed the women
past a beat-up cigar store Indian
into the store's dusty cool
where amber fly strips stirred like streamers
above the sweep of an oscillating fan.

What I didn't understand was how
putting down a person could prop another up.
No one to ask, so instead
I begged Mama for a grape pop.
She hunted for coins as Grandpop strode in
to shoot the shit with the storekeeper.
All hellfire, all brimstone, my grandpop.
In a few years, he'd make one lousy preacher.
He paid for the gas, my grape Nehi.
My love? That went unearned.
I pressed the cold bottle to my chest as I left
but damn if we still didn't burn.

What I Learned Building a House with My Father

Can or can't you
get it right, not bent but perfect—tight
as a chalk line

snapped against wall
or a plumb-bob on a string in pendulous fall?
If not,

the drywall buckles
badly nailed to leaning stud,
or a picture

won't hang right
just because the mark you marked was not true
but bruised

like fruit—the plums
I left out for you, untouched, enduring now
their slow rotting death.

Knowing this
—how easily the things we do go awry—
what can we

expect of truth
when we don't dig for proof
or plumb its depth?

Creation Myth

When my father was more boy than man
        he wanted to live in Greenwich Village but never did.
Kicked out of high school in DC for wearing blue jeans,
        he dreamed of artists and beatniks
            and being the next James Dean.
He moved back to the family farm in West Virginia instead:
        McQuain Road. A mix of dirt and gravel.
Lived in his uncle's house, re-enrolled;
        blue jeans the only trousers country school kids had.
        Hair slicked with Vitalis into a laidback DA,
            white T-shirt, a pack of cigs
                rolled tight in the sleeve—
did he notice my mother's shy locker-side flirt?
Did he question whose hands he'd always been told
        had molded those hillbilly mountains from dirt?

My washerwoman grandmother used to sew
        my mother's dresses from flour-sack cloth.
By high school Mom wore poodle skirts.
            On a neighbor's TV she watched Elvis rock.
        What did she know of a man's shaking hips?
Good girl with good grades, ankles crossed,
                bobby-socked.
        How to crack the cosmic egg?
Separate the raw from the cooked?
        I doubt my mother ever imagined
            her God a feathered serpent
        thinking the world into being,
abstraction into manifestation.
        She was simply dreaming:
church wedding, picket fence. No straining
like Atlas beneath his age-old task
              or a cosmic tortoise—
the world wasn't balanced on a back
              but simple in purpose,
rehearsed: Children the way a girl's singular experience
        stood the chance to become
              multi-versed.

When my father was more boy than man
　　　he wanted to live in Greenwich Village. Never did.
Drafted into the Army instead
　　　　　　　　but kept stateside
painting murals for a nameless colonel's office:
　　　　"The Storming of Iwo Jima", six-foot-by-ten,
　　　　　　　my father's magnum opus.
Discharged,
　　　　　　　he came back to West Virginia.
Drifted awhile, no Moses ready to lead his tribe.
　　　　　　　Trace it to his humble, not heroic, start:
　　　no baby borne down the Nile in a basket,
　　　no alien boy shot through space
　　　　　　like little Kal-El in his speedy rocket.
Dad washed up at Wimpy's Pool Hall instead,
　　　caught the eye of my now more-daring mother.
　　　　　　　Married in May. It rained, I think.
　　　　　　　　　Seven months later came my brother.
　　　By the time I toddled along,
Dad had hung out a shingle as a sign painter.
　　　　　Carwashes. Laundromats—places like that.
My father had long ago become more man than boy.
　　　Greenwich Village lay a lifetime away
　　　　　　　　　　—did he dream of it still?
　　　Summer of Love
　　　　　　　but rent to pay.

My mother became a teacher; it grew clear
　　　　it took more than seven days
　　　　　　　　to create sustainable life.
Still, on Sundays, she placed her tithe
　　　　in a silver plate passed down the pew
while her new baby girl wriggled on her lap
　　　　and her growing boys pulled at their ties
　　　　　　　but kept quiet
drawing pictures of Superman
　　　　　　on the back of empty envelopes.
　　　Dreams were for children,
　　　　　their noses in comics,
　　　　　　　　their heads in the clouds.
　　　Life drew lines, Mom figured out,

14

around what was
                and what wasn't allowed.
No sudden breath of life; no enormous hands
                pulling her up from the dirt.
Only her own hands, her own hard work
                —all ribs remained intact.   Life
could not be shouldered
                                resting on your ass.

At thirteen, I won a contest to read my poems
                at the cultural center in the state cap.
                        A four-hour drive
                through knucklebone mountains.
A workday my parents wouldn't get back.
                In a manila envelope I kept a sheaf of papers
two-finger-typed on my father's Smith-Corona.
                My opus? "A Song for the Whales"
                        and other juvenile crap...I'd not yet seen
                                the ocean. If not for the mountains,
                my earth could have been flat.
Two parents, four kids, all of us dressed
                        not in blue jeans but in our Sunday best,
                and crammed inside
                        a rusted-through
                                blue VW Beetle, February cold
                blasting through the floor. Our hands
                                shivered in our pockets.
Halfway there, I remembered the kitchen table:
                my manila envelope of poems.
Jesus Christ, Dad said when I told him.
                        Can't you make something up?
                He ran his hand through his graying hair,
                        still slicked back in his trademark DA,
                before finally turning the car around.
We made it to the state capital—barely.
                I had my first taste of perfunctory applause.
The real lesson, I know now,
                        was not on stage but in that drive.
                                My parents' pride.
And the way a boy grows slowly curious enough
                to wonder
                        what his world really rests upon.

15

What is the cause of God
                              or anything,
          or is it simply turtles all the way down?
                    Do our parents' dreams hide inside us,
rearticulated, peeping out now and then?
          A brass periscope of their souls' deferment.
It's a miracle our every desire doesn't drive us berserk.
          What are we in search of
                              when we make our little marks?
Creation *ex nihilo*?   No.
          Simply cause and effect,
parents and children,
          and the way time itself is but a lend.

Train Bridge

From hell to high water
the world was ours to steal,
the trestles beneath our feet
tracks where we flattened pennies
under the Chelsea cars' lumbering
weight. Then the river—the water
blinking mud green between the slats
as we stepped out slow, catfish bubbling
the reedy muck below, the wrecked
shopping cart of our lives, the tangled
fishing lines hooked into lips—*I'll never tell,
I swear*—every step forward a dare, and up
ahead the world curving away, one slip
and you could fall, a point made clear
when you pushed me, then grabbed
my elbow in the final second. It would
take me decades to realize you
were so full of shit you'd float
even if I tried to drown you
in snapping turtles, in water,
in the screech and squeal
of a train passing over.

Neighbor Boy

It easily grows bitter, the heart—
a fruit left unripened by kind words, occasional praise.
A hand to tousle a mop of brown hair. A rudder
through boyhood's dangerous days. Seeds
scatter, pecked by birds
with crushable bones and a taste for ruin.
Cruelty becomes a show of strength:
manhood being proven.

ii:

the grieving bone

Antlers

There, among the birches
      in the autumn woods, a faun

         newly welcomed to adulthood's
            lust and bravado.   Too many

         of them again this year—
this one still growing out his antlers,

         the new buds vascularized,
surely warm to the touch,   their velvet

      not yet rubbed away.   Steam rises
         from the faun's freckled shoulders.

In a nearby deer-blind
                  a father whispers to his son:
         Steady. Breathe.
                  Now pull.

         On the long trudge home
the boy learns to shoulder new burdens,
                        surrender beauty
            the way boot steps obscure
                  a track of hooves.

There is a hook in the barn
            and a tub for drained blood.
This year on the door
            they nail a new set of bones.

Ritual

My mother and I find a bat
reeling above our heads the evening we arrive
        with light bulbs
to screw into the ceiling sockets of the half-
        finished home
my father began building before he died:
                the bat startled
by our flung door and blithe conversation,
        my mother and I frozen
among dusty paint rollers and push brooms,
        equally shaken
at the veering path of such sudden
        unexpected flight—like a black scarf
let loose in a stiff, chill wind.
                Hearts calming,
we follow the bat. We formulate a plan:
        a plastic bowl and a small piece
of cardboard to use as a makeshift lid
        so I can trap the tiny body
when, exhausted, it finally alights
        against the ceiling
in the recess of another lightless
        light. A stepladder,
a careful climb. The bat no longer nimble
        but trembling
and looking not so terrible: dustbin fur;
        a faint twitch
among his folded wings' leathery creases—
        strange architecture
I bury beneath my white plastic bowl.
                I slip in
my cardboard lid, press it tight,
        carry the bones and skin
I could break so easily apart
        to the open door my mother holds
and release him. Our bat disappears
        into a sky embroidered
with the first faint stitches
        of the coming night.
My bag's already packed
        and in the car; my mother

21

will have to finish building
this house herself.
In these ways, we rescue ourselves.

No Trespassing

It's no use, the signs she puts up forbidding
four-wheeling teens from joyriding
on the old logging road. No one obeys.
She's always finding clandestine things
when she walks the woods behind her house:
a camp stove where someone was likely
cooking meth. A ladder leading to a deer blind
built in a tree like a child's fort. A deer heart
her dog drags up from where a hunter
gutted his kill. Come summer, it's
a blanket and candles left behind by lovers
whose condom wrappers glint in the filtered light.
The world goes on around her, in the dark,
behind the greens of pine and maple,
when the gift she wants is true silence in her
holler, the wind the only voice whispering
to make her look, her sharp eyes spotting
four-leaf clovers when she lets her dog out to pee.
It's me who worries about her mini-strokes
and falls, the knot on her head from where she
stumbled picking blackberries on the bank.
She watches the bees come, stippling themselves
with pollen, flowers bending in the breeze.
This world is hers, for now—all she covets.
Tonight it is a black bear and three cubs up against
her window, spilling seeds from a bird feeder
hung against the house. My mother stands
in the dark by that window, her thin hand,
the chill of ghostly glass.

Lent

On Ash Wednesday, rain drums a quiet mercy.
John comes home, forehead smudged in a black cross.
A week later, cherry trees bloom in South Philly,
buds fat with wanting though it is not yet spring.
I walk and count each ready shoot: plum, pear,
red tip, daffodil. Already crocuses are spent;
yellow forsythia nearly faded to forget-me-not.

White and pink are whimsies. No time to think—
just be. Sixty-five today, frost tonight, dead blossoms
in the gutter by morning. On the stoop of the bakery
by St. Paul's, a grandfather laughs and lays a match
to a pastel wrapper freed from an amaretto cookie.
All around him, small hands drop crumbs; children stare
bewondered as the fiery paper snakes through the air,
becomes a burst of nothing—no color, not even ash.

Nobody's Savior

Remember our first shared Easter, so warm it was
in our tiny apartment we had to crack the window
while the glazed ham cooked, how we had just enough
time to take a bike ride before your mother arrived,
the two of us pedaling across the South Street Bridge
to West Philly, the view of the city there something I once
painted, back when tall cranes were pushing glass spires
into the sky, the day so warm we took off our shirts,
how on the way back all the things I'd saved myself for
became suddenly pinned to a lone figure—a man standing
too close to the edge, looking like he was going to jump.
And he *was* going to jump, told us so as we neared. I
slowed. Told him no, he didn't want to do that
as I pushed you off to call for help at the 7-11 a block away.

What I talked about to the man I could not tell you now,
only this: the way he knuckle-gripped the balustrade
overlooking the water, the way his lined face looked
pained with worries that I, at 25, could scarcely imagine.
Cars slowed at the strange sight of this white boy and this
black man and the waiting leap that seemed an invitation,
and still a current of words spilled from my tongue
as I tried to stall his intention. Car doors opened, a crowd
gathered, people in Easter finery, a preacher among them
who called out *Brother, you do not want to do this.* I let
the preacher take over, hoping the man could be reached
through prayer and appeals to the Lord. The day was bright
and blossoming and I was a lost key to a lock rusted shut.
By the time you returned with the police, the man had been
rescued, redeemed, led down from the edge, and I felt
cotton-mouthed, spent, vestigial and shaking.

                                        The old bridge
has been replaced in the years since. Its rust scars are gone.
No longer do chunks of concrete fall like fists to the river
and expressway below. The world spins. Your mother is in
a home now. Men still think of jumping. I know.

Walking in Spring Amid a Symmetry of Birch Trees

Inside the mind's illumined dark
        every ribboned thing unfurls:

the thinker foretells
        the way days leave like pages

moss scented, mushrooming
        fiddlehead ferns uncurling
                in the gloaming

        every sapling knowing
time is only loaning you this world

and love is a little blister of venom
        that stings and sings in the veins.

Alien Boy

In San Miguel, two iced tequilas in, my friend
tells me her infant brother died only days after birth.

The announcements were mailed out
despite complications, *It's a boy* trumping fear,

as if hope could ward off an incubator stay
or the vast array of tubes and devices all working

to manage an ailing boy's
breath and blood. My friend's parents rarely spoke

of her brother. Years later, she searched
old medical records to find out what happened.

She sketches me a worry of days:
endless tests proctored, sad looks from nurses,

hushed words of doctors who finally explained
to her parents that among their boy's many problems,

a genital deformity: micro-penis.
Should he live, a choice: flood him with hormones

and raise him a girl, or...?
Or let nature take him as nature nearly had. Should he live?

Their choice? The dice? A nudge?
My friend couldn't say for sure. Who among us could

tell which fear finally exhausts us?
My friend's brother starved from a tube taken out

or perhaps his lungs failed first. Exactitude
is no more recorded than our parents' private words,

choices that might savage an alien boy's
flesh and blood. Any wonder the marriage failed?

Each time a cell divides is a new chance
for the world to go wrong. I'm lucky not to have had to draw

such large lines between loves.
The sun is going down in our Mexican town.

Our drinks are a watery, diluted gold.
I reach to take my friend's hand, think better, and lift my glass instead.

The Lost Boy

All day, the boats look but the search turns up
nothing. That night we sit on the front porch awhile
haloed by citronella candles as a lone truck

combs the lamp-lit streets, spraying
for mosquitos. A three-legged dog
named Lucky roams past, sniffing

the jasmine before continuing his patrol.
How can she bear it, the pitiful woman
who lost her boy to the bay's tricky current?

Who consoles her now? Come morning
we walk to the bay again, wading out
knee-deep, staring farther, as if we might tell

where the steep and sudden drop of the
shipping channel lies. Already the sun throbs
in the sky, while somewhere a mother's sobs

shrivel toward acceptance. We watch
the new day's crowd of beachgoers arrive—
unfolding chairs, fanning blankets—as water

whispers away the last of the boy's story. The depths
of the bay are a church of shadow and light.
After a while, we hotfoot our way across the sand

and back to our rented cottage, where not even
a pitcher of Old-Fashioneds can slake the dryness
in my throat. I know as well as anyone how longing

is a maze that burrows inside us. In the evening
we idle on the porch again, no easy lesson taught.
We breathe in jasmine and wait for Lucky.

Sea Glass

Once vessels, I imagine
—bottles medicine blue,
whiskey brown,

Coca-Cola green—
their sheen in the tidal wash
calls me to collect tiny handfuls

of useless beauty,
bounty burnished by a tumult
of sand & sea

—the way grief
is never done with us
but something that shapes you,

grinds you down to nothing
useful & steals the days
when everyone

pretty & young
was granted clemency
from hard truths.

How many years does it take
to strip away
the soul's entrapment?

Let me be a river
that runs to the sea,
let me be the nothingness

of sea glass
in the sprawling dark,
let the waves call out

o starry womb
vessel unspoken for
contain me.

Uncle

My brother phones to ask a favor,
tells me he's shooting
blanks—his troops too small a tribe

to storm the cervix gate—
glossing with an awkward laugh
his thwarted desire to procreate,

says *So I was wondering, if you'd like, maybe,
donate some sperm*—an idea he tosses out
like bathwater. I hesitate.

He adds, *What? You wanna get paid?*
A joke? A smack in the face?
Meaning double-crosses intention. It has

since boyhood, when we shared a room
but not the private paths
our thoughts, separated, strayed.

Dad's got cancer, my brother reminds me.
You're the only family DNA.
His proposal leaves me flummoxed—

waylaid. I'm balancing miscarriages
against second marriages:
Is it right to create something

that can be taken away?

ii.

I looked at my spunk under a microscope once
back in college when my med-student roommate
brought his new equipment home. Patient, I let him
stethoscope my heart (I had one), take my pulse (it drummed),
before the two of us jerked off onto glass slides
to watch our tadpoles flick like manic commas
as we tuned the scope's lens to 400 MAG.
I felt as close to that roommate as a brother,
told him what a Catholic schoolgirl once said,
how each time a boy masturbates "he spews death
on countless millions" and we laughed at all the times
we'd pleasured ourselves through mass genocide.

iii.

I spend a month thinking of what legal papers
we might draw. I daydream about one of my castaways

alive and rooting inside my sister-in-law.
My son. No, *nephew*.

My *brother's* son—or niece.
I teem with the possibility

of carrying on the family line.
But when I call my brother he tells me

False alarm.
He switched to boxers.

A lab fertilized his wife's egg.
It's growing, alive.

My brother doesn't need me
after all. We can keep on ghosting

through each other's lives. Ten years slip by.
My brother doesn't phone to ask any favors.

He had a boy our father never got to hold.
Our *hellos* and *how-are-yous* are occasional tithes

offered at birthdays and funerals
followed by awkward goodbyes.

Sometimes I see children—
other brothers. The way they wrestle,

bodies sweaty, getting knotted,
steeped in tension and smells

—armpits, peanut butter, sour milk—
until, with a twist, one gets the upper hand:

stronger pins weaker, makes him cry *uncle.*

Siege Engine

Beneath the eaves of the old train depot
I take shelter from a sudden storm,
caught like a crawdad in a plastic cup
—the coolness of the creek bed
my sister and I once plunged our feet in
hot summer days before the sky turned
blue on blue on gray-blue on gray,
and the maples, above, twisted their silvering leaves
as if in astonishment of the coming rain.

> Any kid on our street could tell you:
> rainy afternoons were for swapping stories
> on porch swings. Monopoly marathons.
> The snap of beans in small hands.
> The silken tickle of shucked corn husks
> falling against bare feet. Come evening,
> a Ouija Board might eke out murky futures.
> Or perhaps clearer skies: fireflies in glass jars;
> the naming of constellations.

I knew my sister then like my fingers knew fresh loam,
like my head knew to bury itself in the clean cornflower blue
of a bed sheet drying on a backyard line. Then came time.
No more dancing together among the bright orange whirl
of tiger lilies bobbing in a garden hose's spray. I moved away.
Come home only now and then to watch rain blur to gray
a rusting trestle bridge above the town's brown slip of a river.

> I tell myself I shouldn't fight so much with my sister
> about our aging mother's care. Each trip back,
> more wind-turbines pinwheel on the mountaintops,
> going nowhere. I hate how my heart becomes
> a siege engine here, a system of levers and cantilevers
> and rough ropes I do not understand, never will,
> the way I never manage to find the right counterweight
> to hurl myself back to more balanced days.

Jam

At dusk, they come haunting to slake their hunger:
doe and fawn threading autumn brush. Down hillside,
through hollow, they search for fallen apples—rotten spoils
of the abandoned orchard Mom's lived by since Dad passed on.

The deer move like wood smoke through charcoal shadow;
I'm penciled in against trees, watching roadside, unsure why

a lover once told me he liked me more than raspberry jam
and that—while he loved raspberry jam—he didn't love me.
The truth? I didn't love him either and liked him less
at such clumsy carelessness. So I held my tongue
about his small cock and left with what grace I could muster.

Words are awkward sticky things that sway
from sugar to sour once loosened from tongue.
Do I forgive him because we were young?
Desire reversed doesn't chase need away.

In June, among roadside rock, new blackberries will muster.
Wild strawberries too, budded brambles inviting tongue.
Mom will wash Ball jars before the briars' best
get eaten by deer teaching next year's young. She'll mail me
preserves, knowing—there's nothing I like better than blackberry jam.

But right now, evening drowns in grays and browns. Shadows
swallow me alongside apple, poplar and pine. I'm not sure why

I visit Mom's house more rarely now that Dad is gone.
It feels bruised —an apple fallen and spoiled
beneath the tread of whitetail hooves. Tonight, I prod hillside.
I stay a little longer. I let ache of wanting awaken hunger.

The Grieving Bone

The grieving bone gets lodged in places
other than the heart where one might think

it would fishhook and stay. At night the trains
cut past our coal dark street, the day ahead

as flat as a penny left on the tracks, any promise
of milk and honey gathering like snow

on my father's beard. I had forts to build
and trees to climb. I left my father alone

to nickel and dime away his hours. One summer
night the town roundhouse burned, the heat

blistering the vinyl siding on the houses across
the street. I sat on his shoulders and watched

the smoke spiral, felt the flames dance,
sank my fingers in his hair, not thinking

of futures, his, mine. The sight of him
in a hospice bed would arrive soon enough.

Until then there was the clank and shudder
of metal lumbering in the dark, leaves falling,

the rush of blood in my ears, a ghost train
with nowhere to return, a sharp bone slicing

every part of me.

iii:
bite & balm

The Moon in Drag

Moon of hunger, moon of hope, moon of cold nights
and telescopes. Hunter's moon, low-slung and blood-
orange, moon of fruit and moon of thorn. Mother moon
charming a fussy child, werewolf moon fighting
an urge to go wild. Pale thumbprint sugaring
the afternoon's solid blue, neon moon electrifying
all the night through. Full bellied moon, pregnant
with luck or disaster, moon of witch-chant, halo, antler.
Watercolor moon, soft brushstrokes, wet on wet indigo.
Moon inside me, shifting tides. Moon with thumb out
hitching rides. Witch moon bright behind a claw
of dark branches, skinny-dipping moon, back seats,
taking chances. Up-all-night moon, drinker's moon,
moon of worry and moon of deathbed. Holy moon,
traveler's moon, money tucked in a sock, a comb
in its pocket. Moon we aim for with our rockets.
Crossroads moon where the devil plays his tricks,
junky moon, a sweet stargazer fix. Bake-my-misery-
in-butter-and-brown-sugar moon. Juggler's moon,
bills piled high. Evergreen moon, moon that pines
as cool as creek water, moon of second chances,
moon pressing against the night like a drunken lover,
moon that dances. Moon so blue it is the velvet voice
of a lovelorn swain. Moon so cruel you hope to hide
when it shines this way again. Horse thief moon. Moon
that knows the wind's cold rustle by heart, pained moon,
angry moon, quick and sharp. Moon in feather boas and
come-fuck-me pumps, cinched moon, corseted moon,
moon trussed up to the nines, I'll-have-my-way-with-you
moon that laughs as the willows weep, cricket moon,
lake bottom moon, moon that spoons you as you sleep.

Ruby on Fire

All glitter-bomb the girl with the knobby Adam's apple
she was saving her pennies up to shave down. All eyelash
her eyes, painted big as butterflies when she sized you up
        —I met her bar-backing at Buddies one summer
when I needed extra cash and a kind word thrown my way.
I think she saw a sorrow of birds inside me. I think she thought
I had a broken wing. Ruby performed Fridays, got dressed
in back. My job was stocking beer, washing empties,
hauling the occasional keg, putting up with customers
who squeezed my arms and my ass—even Ruby did it
sometimes as I passed, but I liked how she laughed
with the guardrails off, taught me things I couldn't quite
get my head around, like how to tuck my cock that Halloween
when the whole staff dressed in drag, or the way she
advised me which tricks might be generous, which ones
were creeps to steer clear of.
        Nights at the bar when she sang as Cher or Brittany
she seemed to be made of nothing but sequins and cherry lipstick,
a big wig and an even bigger voice. A dirty hitch to her hips,
and legs to die for slipping through the slit of her flashing gown,
a thick coat of makeup concealing acne scars visible by day,
but man, how she shone in the midnight spotlight
singing on the bar's humble black stage, while all around
human driftwood gathered, Ruby flaming so hot
she sucked up all the oxygen and left us smoldering like embers
when she was done, a superstar for her set
but all nerves and tequila after.
        She showed me her breasts
once her top surgery had healed, her nipples a pair of pink invitations
—I had to stop myself from kissing each one.
        I wasn't there
for her walk home one night, the broken bottle hurled, the teenage
wolves in the car eager for chaos and blood. Eight stitches it took
to sew Ruby's head back together. Half an inch below her wig line
a crescent moon. Life at Buddy's went on until it didn't. I moved on,
thought I fell in love. When I ran into Ruby last, she had changed
her pronouns from she/her to they/them to make clear that if anyone
came at her again she'd be an army of more than just one.
        Burn on, Ruby. Burn on.

A Man in the Station Bar Makes Me Miss My Train

Sit a while, commis—*commemorate*—with a shot to mark the sun's retreat.
I've a bottle of Laphroaig 18, ain't cheap. Plenty peaty. I take it neat, no water.
You kidding me? Men should get to know their poison like Socrates.

Merlot drinker? Ah, that's okay. I prefer shiraz, pinot noir. Good for the heart,
they say—puts blood in the cheeks. Dark glass piles in my recycling each week.
Always one concoction or another to fit life's themes: Work lunch? Rat Pack Martini

—Bombay Gin poured from a sapphire blue bottle. Or Grey Goose vodka—
dirty and shaken; I take it with three olives. I've spent grueling happy hours
at meat markets swilling diluted piss to hold my place, Screwdriver clinking

Fuzzy Navel. I once threw a Cosmo in Carrie Bradshaw's face. Summers
used to mean umbrella drinks inspired by parties or trips. Blue Hawaiian
for misbehaving with a lei around my neck. Or Blood Orange Margaritas...

that beach in Cancun. Fresh lime, muddled mint: Mojitos in Key West.
Back then we drank enough Rum & Coke to fill the Bay of Pigs.
Never did libre Cuba; Castro still ain't dead. My friends are all scattered now

...but I'm getting off-thread. Back to mapping out Mimosa and Bloody Mary
brunch connections. *Drink too much?* Ha! Never. Who am I to defy wise men
or the gods before me, to abstain from the nectar this young Ganymede is pouring?

But I'm keeping you. The hour's late. The kitchen staff smokes in the alleyway.
Bear me out. One more. No doctor complaints; think of Prometheus instead: Livers
regenerate. So here's to champagne for new jobs, new houses, new babies on board,

and sometimes just for days I don't call in dead. Where'd my roaring twenties go,
my wild grad-school nights? The beer kegs are emptied; Mad Dog's been put down
like whiskey in Guinness: Irish Car Bomb suicide. I said *sit*. A dram for freshman year!

When underage I still managed to drink the bottom shelf dry. Fake ID, three bottles of
Boone's Farm for a five. Add a pizza from Domino's, stir in a reggae beat, and before
I knew it we were all cock-deep in Dionysian throes, though not even that compares

to high school stolen six-packs, PBR's quench, and cheap Riunite brown-bagged
on park bench. The very first drink I ever mixed? Grape Kool-Aid plus an ounce snuck
from every house on Locust Street. A cocktail for a slumber meet. Purple Jesus—get it?

Grape tongue stain, middle-of-the-night upchuck refrain: *Jesus, sweet Jesus, never again.*

Waitress: Tennessee Diner, 1974

In my new-linen days, hope climbed through me,
a wisteria vine whose bloom wouldn't come.
I was young, easily tamed,
laying out nice suppers nights he got home.
And ironing blue work shirts,
his name stitched to the chest,
as if either of us could forget who we'd become.
Any novelty was short-lived, a let's-pretend game
like the feeder of sugar water
I hung on the porch of our rented trailer
and forgot about when no hummingbirds came.

The name now pinned to this pink uniform
is not who I used to be. That other self
I left in West Virginia like the hand-me-down bed
I slept in when I fooled myself into believing
I knew what love was:
a soldier-boy old enough to buy a girl beer,
with bottle-brown eyes that hammered my heart
and fists not yet ignited.
Yes, I got out from under Mama's thumb
but became a rabbit lost in a warren of my own making.
I can still see his Pall Mall cindering our bedroom's dark
—his every drag burned his cheekbones bright
as his eyes held on to their twin scoops of shadow.
He crushed out his cigarette and then crushed me
beneath an ashen kiss and a too-powerful need.

I laid out nice suppers nights he came home
and even nights he didn't.
Told myself there'd come reprieve,
trusted God to visit.
But the doctor just looked at me funny
the day I told him I tripped taking in the mail.
Your baby, he said in the clinic's hard light,
would have been a girl.
Five days later, I caught the only bus out of town,
slunk down low in my seat
as we passed the station where he worked,
and the factory, nearly as empty as the church.
My dead cousin's birth certificate

brushed my thigh like a man's hand.
I had it pinned inside my skirt.

Those days are an empty closet with no note;
these days are a back-aching abacus of safety.
Still I don't complain.
Each shift picked up is a promise to myself:
Never again.
Night truckers who come in, I can handle.
Didn't take me long to pad these girls for better tips.
Ten years and my arches still hold up
against this concrete floor skimmed with vinyl.
Watch me flirt, pour your coffee, jot down your order.
Whole wheat or white with your breakfast special, honey?
I've learned life's lingo.
Everything's scrambled in the end.
I call it to the cook, who thinks he knows what I'm saying:
One Adam and Eve on a raft and wreck 'em.

Although Their Eyes Were Kind

(a remix of Shakespeare's sonnet 69)

Southern boys with guns from fathers' cases
lie in wait to send friends to dreamless sleep.
Their hearts disregard shocked looks on faces.
This world is full of mothers who now do weep.
To look inside a pimply killer's heart for proof
we might expect to find neglect, abuse.
What love toward others in that chest does sit?
We want to know these ruffians lack some part
—yet wrath seldom provides such easy excuse.
It is in fear that children now do lie
beneath lunch tables out of sniper range.
And if, by chance, head raised, they should die
look to a classmate for this death arranged.

The Absinthe Drinker

It's clear he's hit the road
—a Kerouac, a Hemingway—

leather journal, expensive camera,
t-shirt from the Kafka Café.

He struts in, sits beside me,
asks the bored barkeep to set him up:

etched glass, silver spoon, cube of sugar on top
over which acid-green absinthe is poured

drop by drop. In broken English
the Czech barkeep starts to instruct—

the young American waves him off,
doesn't want to hear it. He's got a guidebook,

knows all about this stuff. He clicks his lighter,
sets the soaked sugar afire. Spoon plunge,

quick swirl. His glass glows—a blue flame—
and before the barkeep can translate or I can explain

douse or *blow out* the kid drinks it down.
The scent of fennel and anise collapses

into a stench of burnt hair. The kid's eyebrows gone now.
At least he's still got his eyes. I pound his back

as he coughs into the bar. Our barkeep no longer bored
but raising an eyebrow in a way my new friend

can't anymore. *Stupid kid*, I think
as I signal us a second round. The two of us

both flotsam. This rainy day. This bar. So I listen
to my younger version blame all his folly

on the green fairy's hallucinogenic effects.
Only stopping over in Prague, he tells me.

Running with the bulls is next.

Mechanical Bull

Tonight he feels the need for a strange word
        in his head: *lepidopterist* perhaps
        ("studier of butterflies and moths")
        or *callithump* (discordant parade;

secondary meaning: "burlesque serenade").
        This queer honky-tonk he's come to
        verges on colony collapse disorder
        and he is wingless, friendless,

whiskeyed thoughts abuzz
        in a droning moment that isn't metaphor
        but clinking with beer bottles
        while drag queens and good old boys

two-step over peanut shells on sawdust floors.
        Tonight he has no patience
        to puzzle himself apart. Rodeos like these
        require a different kind of smart:

something more than rough rope to grab
        as he climbs aboard the beast's back—
        where, with a flicked switch, time deconstructs
        into a series of jerks and false starts:

Old boyfriends? First loves?—fools fit
        to leave in the past. He holds onto
        strange words as this mechanical beast bucks:
        calli—what the hell—*thump?*

He is here because he knows he is drowning too much
        in bougainvillea on white walls,
        watershed memories, the wild rush
        of all of life's stimuli

passing through myopic eyeball lens—*too fast!*—
        he holds onto strange words,
        these little reinventions of his world; he grabs at
        this house-mix of testosterone,

sawdust shavings, Stetson cologne, while beneath him
        the mad bull leaps and dives and the drag queens
        on the sidelines bat their butterfly eyes.
        He holds onto strange words the way he holds close

his need to be freed—tight, as if gripping the universal cock
        creating life. Still the world gets in,
        meaning wrung from being—
        doesn't matter a damn he can't sort

his newsfeed. Is he rider or bull now? Bucked
        or fucked? It's only a mechanical bull,
        itself a metaphor, the way love sometimes is
        a bee trapped in a real bovine's silken ear:

stinging, nettlesome, too much to bear. "Will attract
        butterflies and bees" the seed catalog read.
        But the bougainvillea didn't take.
        This hive's nearly dead. And the lepidopterist?

He doesn't yet have tonight's butterfly pinned
        among the bow-tie rows in his shadowbox.
        Somewhere a lone moth slo-mo struggles
        beneath a chloroform cloth, while our rider

puffs his spirit, holds on, clings to strange airs;
        he crams his brain with ten-dollar words:
        oleaginous (covered in grease),
        batrachophagous (eater of frogs)—anything

to lift his spirits from the muck of the mulligrubs.
        How are we reformed and into whom?
        Maybe our lepidopterist is on lidocaine.
        Our bull throws our rider into an embrace

of hoots and jeers. Like a word giving up its meaning.
        Like a world giving up on meaning.
        Meaning? We all ride our own bull,
        both mechanical and real. So let our cowboy

think in terms of drowning too much.
        Now, on the floor as he picks himself up
        he can hear his mother reciting from a picture book:
        "*Oh, oh, the places you'll go!*" Hand him his hat.

Time to rodeo.

Two Girls in West Philly Spray Their Hair into Beehives

They are the summer's buzz and the chill
of cold forties pressed to the sweaty
crooks of their knees, pretty as a pair
of hip-hop princesses dressed up in thrift shop
finery. Tonight they are golden, all honey
and shiver, and sweet clover perfume
as the moon peeks out. Honeysuckle
and lavender, clever and bawdy,
they're here to kick the door in
to the after party. Their lips are glossed,
aglow like lightning bugs, their hair
is teased as high as the rafters. They're
ready for business if that business
is pleasure. Tonight they're the girls
every man here is after. They've unlocked
the laughter from their private
honeycombs, sugared old hurts
till they taste like Alizé. They sparkle,
they shimmer; friends find them
unfamiliar; they dance with each other,
push drunk men out of the way. Tonight
someone's tagging the overpass again;
someone's got hotdogs sizzling on a grill.
Someone's spilling cheap gossip
that stings like 80 proof. None of it matters
to these two kissing girls.

New Jersey Naiad

Let the mind compose its square of sky,
define your disguise, a murder of crows
distilled to flapping black passing by—
caw and claw raking cornfield now
near Pine Barren roosts and the slow
meandering sluice of tannin-stained
river water. If there still were nymphs,
if there still were daughters of wood,
water and sky, where would they roost—
roadside among temporary tomato stands
or on rusty flatbeds saddled with apples
picked by migrant hands? Would they
convene, perhaps, in a canoe rental shack
among webby shadows and paddles
stacked loosely in back?
Where asphalt gives way to gravel we've come,
slathered in sunblock, trying on
lifejackets until we find the one that fits;
then we board a school bus, repurposed
so bodies can learn a dirt road's grammar
of potholes and bumps. Soon the cool woods
and waiting water. The lost impossible
daughter. Steady the boat, enter—
the world disassembles. Tremble.
Just now you've once again caught her.

Snake

It is a green snake the boy finds. No rattler.
No copperhead like the one his father killed
the summer before

in the dirt road by the one-room schoolhouse,
bramble-covered & abandoned,
wild strawberries blooming

through the wooden shambles. A grass snake.
Harmless, found among sunflowers,
nothing worth knowing

a machete's blade. The snake twines
through the boy's hands. He tries to calm
its twisting coolness. No copperhead

coiling among tree shadows in a dusty road,
no poison, only something to sneak
into a bedroom. A secret. Nothing

worth knowing its own blood, only hands,
a hot summer & a road so far from town
as to be entirely untethered

by sidewalks, telephone lines, asphalt.
The road slips around the world
like a snare, slips around time

—until you are a man watching a boy
watching a snake on a dirt road untethered
by telephone lines, asphalt,

grace. Standing as if shackled
in a room full of horseflies
and no words. And the room

is the world, and here is a boy:
See him now, walking a dirt road
with his father.

Glass Frog

Hyalinobatrachium ruedai

At first the glass frog's skin
seems torn away, a gelatinous membrane
unadorned, little to her

but lime green glaze.
What if invisibility worked this way?
Translucence limited

to just our skin—a sudden
peepshow of what lies within like the
plastic human anatomy kit

I used to play with
as a kid. Would we love what we see
or find it grotesque? The fat

around viscera; meat
slow to digest in a stomach that sits inches
beneath a glass-

encased heart
stripped of symbolism to mechanical beat?
I'd like to think

we'd find eloquence
in any self magicked, imagined. Or overlooked
as easily as

a ghost-skinned,
almond-sized frog on a leaf—bejeweled by her
organs pulsing beneath.

Annabelle

she sits near the bus driver to avoid abuse
worse than a lunchbox's metal edge
thrust forward   her ample hip
meaty bruise of all yesterdays.

black pirate patch our easy target, fat-hammed heart
an easy mark   that lazy eye
sees barbs no better than her
daddy's hands moving in the dark.

in Science, gravity's rudiments offer no
makeshift rules to explain dodgeball
collisions of men and skin
night's rough impact, cooties and all.

(animal magnetism gives way to magnets
on refrigerators, more chins,
consolatory ice cream
cools blunt bruise, nitey-nite dribbles)

bathrooms stall-less, she fears to squat among static
clean virginity   panties proof
she's daddy's good girl special
won't let it show, won't let it seep.

inside, her skin leeches invisibility
flesh unflinched by ages battered
organs pump beneath each bruise
guardian angel home sick, tattered.

fourth period passes, lunch and Social Studies,
she chews on paste to knot herself
won't seep,   glues what knickers know
elastic bites, his touch burns deep

> *flush out his touch, he touched her*
> *shout out he touches, he touched her*
> *even now he touches, he touched her*
> *must hold the touch, he touched her*

bladder breaks baby's bough, sinking shame on plastic
new fame unfolds fresh ridicule
deep-seated chair and county
carpet.   Against her will she had to mark it.

Mercy

The Hell's Angel claimed to have died
                    in Death Valley, aptly enough,
when his motorcycle slid out from under him:
          loose rocks on hot highway asphalt,
                    a sudden swerve and a sideways skid
that nearly undid him.
                         Lying then
                    in the hot desert sun
where shadow birds would soon come
          to make new feathers from the pluck and pull
of his meat.   Instead:
                    a miracle of paramedics
to stanch his blood, to brace his neck
          —red sirens screaming for miles—
and a swelling in his head.   A heart that flat-lined
for six minutes on an operating table
                         —but man,
what that Hell's Angel learned in that eternity of time
—and now
          here to share it with my high school class,
thanks to a hippie English teacher and a visitor's pass,
the Good News there was a Heaven
                    even for Hell's Angels.
I listened to him tell us
     in his beer-breath-and-cigarette way
          how we lived in a universe
                    of infinite grief and loss
          —and grace—
where earthly ignorance equaled fear,
                                   where fear
equaled hate. But after death, that transitive equation
          no longer held sway.   Imagine:
no lost souls, no loners anywhere
          —only a place   outside of time,
               where those who did wrong
realized the wrong they had done
                         and were absolved,
released from the damnation
                         I'd always been taught
—locked in that furnace boiler of church and youth—
               was fitting retribution

for all the evil
            mankind had done   or would ever do.
My heart fumbled over itself,
                            a football I couldn't catch.
                    A force of grace freed from wrath?
I couldn't fathom it, had to ask:
                                        "Even Hitler?"
"Even Hitler,"
                smiled our leather-jacketed guest lecturer
through a stubbly face still scarred by stitches.
At fifteen,
            I had a hundred Hitlers
                                    sinning inside me
and needed angels with fiery swords
                                    to do my dividing.

Tonight, as I write this,
                Reverend Fred Phelps lies on his death bed,
the Westboro Baptist preacher
            who dared mock a beaten boy
crucified and left for dead.   Matthew Shepherd:
                Can you picture him—bleeding,
        tied to that cold Wyoming fence?
            I'm sure Phelps raised his sign,
                        GOD HATES FAGS,
far more over the years
                    than I raised SILENCE = DEATH.
The plague stole friends
                —Charles, Peter, Harvey—
left me body-shaped outlines
                        chalked on asphalt at die-ins.
Forgiveness is a virtue, yes
                    —but it's a shiv that comes in slant.
Reverend Phelps, as he dies, had better pray
        Hell's Angels show him grace.   I can't.

Night Birds

When I find I doubt my purpose,
and my scant faith weaves and waffles,
the weight of this life undermined
by fear of what might come to be—
When my body cannot escape
the judgement of its labors
and I creak and groan
like the riddled wood that shores me—
I look to the evening sky,
at the stars there, being beautiful,
and forget for a moment the unalienable fears
that knot my tangled observations.
I dream of constellations not yet named,
of ghosts, in reprieve, sent ascatter—
I invite the night birds to invent new songs
inside the empty house of my soul.

Tonight Guanyin Seeks an End to Suffering

First have her born a boy
        in lotus petals unfolding,

growing in need & wanting
        an end to wanting   —but oh, if only

the blessing of his body's skin
        could glide, silken

as an older sister's dress, stolen,
        tight & white, flowing over him now

like water,   spilling him
        into a sacred vase

of another self.   Let him become
        a vessel that knows

how to hold & succor,
    let him assume   the form want needs.

This is how a young man
        becomes a Mary

anything but virginal:
        Guanyin

strutting in stiletto heels
        beneath October street lamps, cutting

a slender silhouette   among headlights
    sharking by.   *Mámá*

and *bá's* South Philly walk-up
        might as well be as far as China—

as far as every star unseen, gazing down now
        at this boy becoming

all gesture & fierceness,   all bite & balm.
        A flip of the hair, a bat of smoky lashes:

Tenderness.   Tonight
         gender will be no obstacle

to enlightenment.   Guanyin will bend
         like a willow branch   to their bodies,

let them inside   as a boy is reborn
         into a goddess of mercy:

fingers in her mouth now & her ears filled
         with all this world's

heaving lamentations.   Even if it takes
         a thousand arms, a thousand eyes

to save them from their suffering,
                she will be their Bodhisattva

forgoing nirvana's bliss.   In her arms
     she holds   mothers whose children

disappear,   fathers whose cars
         cruise city streets,   all the ungodly

little boys & girls,   the in-betweens
         waiting to transform into truer selves,

locked at this moment, asleep & dreaming
         inside the heart of a lotus flower.

iv:
tin hearts

Tongue

The tongue I try to master
is a sticky one, forked and full of tricks,

risking collision of sense and nonsense
—recompense for a fractured age.

I am beyond murmuring. Neologisms
abound in your body, and I plan to master

the patois of each part, learn where bones divide
like syllables. Feel my fingers on your ribcage

catching your barrel-chested bellows;
feel my hand against your throat

waiting for words to come. For I calculate
the onomatopoeia of your longing

in all its sibilants and sweet susurration.
Let me hiss it back to you—a viper;

let me lap your words awhile—a vampire.
Too long we have cyphered our desires.

This tongue I try to master is yours, mine,
ours. Speak to me in its unspoken language

as our fingertips brush each other's beards,
trigger arousal. For I covet the divot

in your chin, the muscled flex of your jaw,
your parting lips, wet, and now revealing

the subtle diastemic divide in your teeth
so faint I have to move even closer to see.

Teach me what lies beneath meaning.
Tell me in your body's heat, its blood,

its breath, its need—rising now
like a shiver, a stutter, an unuttered word

buried beneath this kiss: first taste
of the tongue I master.

.

Constellation

Trace a consequential motel room:
glow of anonymous light,
perfect sphere of a moment when
you first shared scars, introduced wounds,
thinking they might heal or melt you
—stars of sugar on the tongue.

You took off your clothes, started to
put them back on—a Möbius striptease.
Where to begin to love someone? So much
to do and never enough hands
to beat back blood or pin wonder to a face.

You stole new ground, saw the shadow
of a hawk, wondered how to outrun
time together. Whose tongue to use?
You were different languages, newly minted,
men flawed and freckled—awash with lines
there would never be maps enough to chart.

Monkey Orchid

Orchis simia

"Found throughout southern Europe as well as the Mediterranean, Orchis simia, the Monkey Orchid, is remarkable at under twenty-four inches for its speckled clusters of purple-pink blooms. Each flower is simian-shaped and complete with what can best be described as an engorged monkey 'phallus'—thus necessitating this orchid be kept far from the bouquets of impressionable young ladies of genteel upbringing."
— Lord Basil Attenborough, *A Field Guide to the Flowers and Grasses of Western Europe*. London, 1899

"Trust me."
— Circuit party. New York City, 1999

Tonight I'll wear my joy
    erect, conspicuous and speckled,
        opening a turnstile
to a tumble of tribal brothers
    clanging cymbals, clinging arms,
while what dazzles
      dangles
          for all to see—
so let's dance!
    Shoulder the weight
      of our bodies' burdens,
    fling our funny crap,   laughing
as a mirror ball sequins our skin:
      We are locked in a roving sea
of sweaty chests and clamoring hands
    each of us waving our Day-Glo glans
      ornamentally, raving
    to a techno-beat.   You, me?
We blend into one   ecstasy,
    an orgy of blossoms,
      of bottoms and tops
living as if we will always be
    a party to the circuit party
      —a parable of pleasure
almost parody.

Tonight   I am scared
and electrified by everything I could become:
      pure monkey desire,
                my cock a loaded gun
      blossoming on this shared stamen
of desire
        —don't think of disease—
      We are   a monkey orchid
seeking release
          from mostly awkward
     daytime moments
         that drive us half-insane,
surrounded now by similar selves,
         drugs dreaming in our veins.
      Tonight   I am sacred:
watch me unfold:
     a wallflower at the orgy growing bold.
Are these spots on our skin
     the blotchy purple-pink of sexual flush?
Amyl-nitrate on our breath,
         a popper-bottle head rush.
     Each lick
      is like a whisper
         not quite confessional
as our bold stamens keep unloading
      in this strobe light processional
of desire aping love,
     of young men exploding, all the while
our secret saner selves
      haunted, wondering:

        Will we survive
this ravenous age of plague
     when blood wants to become
          one river running
      through many bodies?
    Oh, we playful, foolish monkeys.
Oh, this petal cage of desire and death.
     Kiss me quick—first you, then you—
as I bare my teeth
      and keep barreling through.

Thirst

From Mexico I brought you a silver and red heart:
                              a tin *corazon* to decorate our Christmas tree.
            And after a night in a luckless bar—*El Gato Negro*—
a cocktail recipe: tequila and grapefruit soda—*Poloma*,
            the Spanish word for 'dove', the same pale name
as the stubborn horse I rode
                                          through Guanajuato
without you by my side.

                                    I don't know what I drank
that other night, an even unluckier bar in old San Miguel.
            Tecate? Negra Modelo? Some other cheap local beer?
La Cucaracha—the Cockroach dive that would not die,
            where Beats like Kerouac and Cassidy loved and fought.
And where local drunkards sighed at my American jibes
            as doe-eyed *jotos* sized me up from the back wall.

I missed you then, like I did this summer in Shanghai
            on wild Nanjing Road drinking Heinekens with a Hawaiian
named Billy, who never met a bottle of *baiju* he didn't like
            —it helped him chase hookers along the city's neon strip.
Baiju: rotgut Chinese white lightning distilled from sorghum,
            barley or millet. One swig from Billy's tiny green bottle
and I quickly had my fill of it.

            Never brought any home from the trip   —only stories:
of strange fruits, fried scorpions, whiskered fish.
            Of the giant Buddhas carved from the Yungang Grottoes,
of the ancient monastery clinging to the Hengshan cliffs.
            I climbed the Great Wall, sang karaoke in Pingyao,
made a friend or two over a bottle of scotch—but for three weeks
            among strangers in dirty coal-burning country
                              it wasn't just blue sky I missed.

                              On my way home
I bought you a bottle of Crown Royal from Toronto,
            duty-free and flavored with maple,

because I liked to imagine the sight of you in your boxers
bringing pancakes to our breakfast table.
Something new to slake your thirst, I said,
handing the brown bottle over.
You told me to add ice cubes and keep the drink simple:
"We'll call it a Mrs. Butterworth."

These days,
it seems I'm always returning from somewhere far off,
even if it's just back to our conversation at the table.
Our lives drink up the years, I want to say.
They burn like a dragon, they sing like a dove.
Don't hate me because I can't keep still
and need to fill my cup up to the brim—
I'd drink your heart right now if I could,
even if it were silver
and red
and made of tin.

How an Owl Spins Its Head Without Tearing Apart

The human neck is a delicate pulsing stem,
pretty but poorly made. Torque or twist too much
and carotid or vertebral arteries might tear.

There's no safe way to take the world entirely in,
now in the pines as a branch dips and rises
releasing to the air an unseen wingéd heft:

a silhouette moving fast, like the idea of itself,
flying above our clumsy, slow-turning heads.
On a night that has already offered an exchange

of starlight for the erasure of a barn's bright red,
where an owl hoots now: surely he sees us,
as skittish as field mice, as he spins his neck:

arteries widening into reservoirs, not narrowing,
the further blood travels from his quick-beating heart.
I wish that I were made such a way: unafraid,

unmasked. Able to drink you in without splitting apart.
Tonight these woods are astir with words unsaid:
how I'd risk my neck to swoop you up from this dark.

Rain in Old Movies

that summer when art school purchases
     reduced your wallet's contents to atoms

and Raman noodles
     were for dinner again

        unable to afford surcharges at ATMs

temp work in a tie all day
            easily unknotted, replaced
by happy hours richly steeped
       in meaning-of-life conversations

you: a wet-eared country mouse
        in the big city
standing shoulder to shoulder among new friends

     taking delight in random misdirection
or the buddy who let you borrow five bucks
     for a cheap pitcher of beer at Dirty Frank's bar
       to chase away rot-gut whiskey shots

       you laughed and bitched
   and bristled
      at the world's imperatives,   art
the religion that might save you

     content to let the day take you into night
        oil paint beneath your fingernails
no windows curtained
      in this hard-knock education
where you were slowly learning to unlearn
       and when to leave well enough alone

dawn was a crippled victory not yet fought
     on those near-unbearable August nights
when desire was an uncanny lunar succulent
     that only grew harder the worse the drought got

     experience was the drug you were after:
the need to be high enough to cruise and hook up
      with anyone who had working AC

your body, a lovely commodity
as you gamboled through desire and disease
        the way high rollers gambled in Atlantic City

what did you learn?   wisdom
        was a cut that healed stronger than its wound;
            regret left sun enough to always re-bloom

and come the morning's inevitable walk of shame
                    a sudden downpour
            of summer rain
        left you grinning, wanting more

such memories, full color, fade
        into nostalgia-tinged
            sepia-toned black and white;
        you never know you're in a golden moment
            until time's hand flicks out the light

was it ever once so easy,
        desire hinging on a partner well-hung?
            every discovery
                    as sweet as sin—*how alive*
    and living you were then!—
in the grand movie of being young

Memory Is a Taste That Lingers on the Tongue

On St. John, the high island winds
unwound us after a day of too much sun—
our beach things tucked in our rental car's trunk

as we swerved the hillside hairpin turns
and jounced past scrambling Billy goats.
Down to town we drove: the docks

of Cruz Bay beleaguered by tourists; the streets
bottlenecked with cars from the ferry
spilling past whitewashed shops and houses

drowning in late sun and the purples and pinks
of frangipani, bougainvillea, hibiscus.
On the docks we found a bare-chested fisherman

gutting the day's catch, his graying dreadlocks
slung down his back as he pressed his knife
into a fat red snapper. Another lay upon the dock,

its gills still fighting against the world's air.
While the fisherman worked we haggled for the pair
before finally acquiescing to his stubborn price.

He wrapped the fish, laid down his knife.
Our hands brushed in the exchange
of money for a meal. Later we cooked those fish

in our windy house as the sun went down
and the moon came out. Lights flickered inside
sailboats anchored in the little bay below.

Even now I can taste that red snapper in my mouth.

Two Hymns

Bending, baring all, could make two hymns become one
as if bare-knuckle boxing were an act of love or turning,
the whistle of an age hammering the sky full-force.
Something must break—a heart, a neck—
in order to survive. It's 1965, and like anything transported,
it passes. Each knows he must transcend himself:
two hymns, no refrain. The other's turn. A train.
A knotted string passes up and out of him,
locked rock solid, then shaking, buckling, pinioned
like wings, he thinks—or is it him? Legs: they become
a dark machine, sweetly pistoning, against bare
buttocks, the night as chilly as ice water. Together
the stubble of jaw-lines, insistent as a rush of air. Here:
what only men can do. Crushed grass prickling trouser
knees. He is wanting him wanting him, bound now in sin.
The younger trembles. An open mouth the leaked proof.
A stroke of the face, a hand on a chest. The older bends;
their bodies a cavernous depot of desire,
grazing mouths that can never touch bottom. Mutual
wonder at whether the other will do all he needs him to,
fit as a soldier—two hymns, parts played in equal measure.
Two hims: one weathered, gray, the other young, a kindly
commerce of the flesh, cellular, it is so essential
carried on a shocked exhalation of breath—desire—
quiet hymns, made of fear and gratitude, a close moment
when they might feel beautiful, a place to float to, town
forgotten. A canopy of stars, no scythe to cut the high grass
low. Two hymns interlace where such men idle.

Fireworks

Honeysuckle lingers in the air like it can survive
our futures. The last of the sun purples from the sky.
We have paused, awaiting something—not the scent
of hay and horses from the neighbors' farm,
nor the moon, aglow, inching above a dark silo. Yes,
we have crumbed our tablecloth, spit watermelon seeds
in sticky contests, and all our friends' not-quite-goodbyes
linger in the wings like fireflies soon to be trapped
in the bell jar of the past. Tonight the sky is an open
page, a watchful spell, an incantation in calm indigo—
where all the coming chinks in our armor seem, somehow,
serenely guarded, under a parent's watchful protection:
a babe at peace asleep in his stroller dreaming his luck
never ends. Tonight we're happy to be alive
in these early owl-less hours, forgetting lost jobs,
howls of childbirth pain, which bills to pay, the slipperiness
of rain. We exist solely beneath the constellations'
weightless gaze, the thimble-light of a citronella candle
the only thing we need to handle all our earthly
insect cares. Let the amber comfort of a passed bottle
warm our bones down to the marrow, warding off
the gathering chill. Here. Help me carry these blankets
down to the dock to wait, arm in arm, for fireworks
(*o glittering dahlia! o luminous aster! may you shield us
from disaster!*). Let's remember when time was a blur
ripe with possibilities, when our bodies had not yet
settled into these all-too-human forms, when night
might gently howl to remind us there is still in us all
                    a bit of starlight,   feather,   fur.

Strawberries, Limoncello, Water Ice, Passing Time

You bring home Italian Market strawberries
so ripe they'll be ruined if we don't eat them today

so after dinner I wash, core and halve them
as you water plants off the deck, the last of the sunlight

purpling the sky. I drop the strawberries
into a bowl over lemon water ice,

add a shot of *limoncello* from a bottle given us
last Christmas, carry the bowl and two spoons

up to our bedroom, trying not to dig in
before you join me for a movie. But I can't;

it's too good, so sugary, so cold, while the day's been
so hot we ate dinner without shirts. I can taste

fresh lemon peel in the homemade *limoncello*
as if Christmas were yesterday, not half a year ago.

I pluck a strawberry from the bowl and study it close
as the water shuts off and you curl away the hose—

such scarlet skin, so many tiny seeds, every one
a wonder. My fingers redden with juice,

grow sticky-sweet with water ice. When you come in
I pop the strawberry in my mouth, a guilty child,

thinking of a sunburn long ago,
how you rubbed my skin aloe-cool, and then

rubbed me again, stirring blood, ripening stamen
until I seeded red skin and took safety in

the false comfort there would be time enough
for everything. Our bed creaks as you crawl in.

You fluff your pillow; I spoon you water ice and
a strawberry half, its white V within—this moment

a victory. A drip hits my chest and you tongue it away.
What flavor is inside ourselves?

Sweetness, surely, the way you lap at my heart—
like strawberries, *limoncello*, water ice, passing time.

Torn

At first, it's only a hoof where my left foot
used to be, and the only inconvenience

is a shoe that won't fit. But then, overnight,
a nagging migraine builds to a hard nub

that sprouts five inches above my left eye—
worse than teenage acne: a *horn*

my hairline can't disguise. Left eyebrow, too,
is acting up—arching, turning black—

to match half a goatee below—I shave it off;
it re-grows. The hair on my left leg

feels coarser, and now my leg is bending
—goat's hock curving to fetlock. Won't straighten,

it kicks back! Tail's the worst; it's forked
—a bit furry, a bit skinned—darting now

through a hole in my boxers. I decide
to call in sick. And it's true, I'm in agony:

left shoulder blade wrenching, a loud snap.
On my back, a black umbrella unfolds

into a leather wing. In the mirror, half a devil
and I wonder whether hope might spring

from my other side. First sign: a feather.

Notes

"Creation Myth"—"Creation *ex nihilo*" refers to a Latin phrase, *creatio ex nihilo*, meaning the creation of something out of nothing. The expressions "cosmic tortoise" and "turtles all the way down" allude to the idea of the World Turtle and comes in particular from an apocryphal story about a well-known astronomer (possibly Bertrand Russell) who was giving a lecture describing how the earth revolved around the sun and how the sun orbited around the stars of our galaxy. *In A Brief History of Time* (1988), author Stephen Hawking describes the scene just so:

> *At the end of the lecture, a little old lady at the back of the room got up and said: "What you have told us is rubbish. The world is really a flat plate supported on the back of a giant tortoise." The scientist gave a superior smile before replying, "What is the tortoise standing on?" "You're very clever, young man, very clever," said the old lady. "But it's turtles all the way down!"*

"Mercy"—Attorney Fred Waldron Phelps Sr. (1929-2014) achieved nationwide notoriety as pastor of the Westboro Baptist Church, a hate group known for their extreme views against homosexuality. He led numerous protests at the funerals of gay people, military veterans, and disaster victims—people he believed were killed as a result of God punishing the U.S. for tolerating homosexuality. One such target was murdered University of Wyoming college student Matthew Shepard (1976-1998), who was beaten, tortured, and left to die tied to a barb-wire fence outside Laramie, Wyoming. Shepard's murderers, Aaron McKinney and Russell Henderson, were convicted in 1999 with each sentenced to two consecutive life terms.

"Tongue" leapt from a reworking of a line from Abena Busia's poem "Caliban" ("This tongue that I have mastered").

Acknowledgments

Grateful acknowledgment is given to the editors of the following publications where these poems first saw print, some in slightly different form:

A&U Magazine: "Monkey Orchid"
American Poetry Review and *Best New Poets 2000*: "The Moon in Drag"
BLOOM: "Alien Boy," "Brave"
Blue Lyra Review: "Strawberries, Limoncello, Water Ice Passing Time"
Book of Matches: "Nobody's Savior"
Codex Journal: "Architect"
Connotation Press: An Online Artifact: "The Absinthe Drinker"
Emerge: 2015 Lambda Fellows Anthology: "Fireworks"
Fox Chase Review: "Ritual"
Gay and Lesbian Review Worldwide: "Neighbor Boy"
Grand Journal: "The Lost Boy," "Snake"
jmww: "Siege Engine," "Southern Heat," "Uncle"
Kin: "Torn"
Knockout Magazine: "Mercy," "My Father's Shop"
Lambda Literary Review: "Tongue"
Limp Wrist: "Dolly," "Ruby on Fire" (the latter selected by Dorianne Laux as winner of the magazine's inaugural Glitter Bomb Award)
Mead: "Lent"
Mount Hope Literary Magazine: "How an Owl Spins Its Head Without Tearing Apart," "Walking in Spring Amid a Symmetry of Birch Trees"
Philadelphia City Paper: "Annabelle"
Philadelphia Stories: "Thirst," "Two Girls in West Philly Spray Their Hair into Beehives"
Paper Nautilus: "New Jersey Naiad"
The Pinch: "Waitress: Tennessee Diner, 1974"
Press 1: "Constellation"
Redivider: "Camping as Boys in the Cow Field" (selected by Reginald Dwayne Betts as winner of the magazine's AWP Quickie Poetry Contest)
Rogue Agent: "The Grieving Bone"
Spunk: "Two Hymns," "Tonight Guanyin Seeks an End to Suffering"
Stone Highway Review: "Annabelle"
Weave: "What I Learned Building a House with My Father"

Some of these poems were also published in two suites of poems in the Sibling Rivalry Press journal *Assaracus*. Issue 10: "Alien Boy," "Lent," "Glass Frog," "Torn," "Jam," "New Jersey Naiad," "Strawberries, Limoncello, Water Ice, Passing Time." Issue 18: "Ritual," "Camping as Boys in the Cow Field," "Antlers," "Architect," "Monkey Orchid," "Thirst," "What I Learned Building a House with My Father."

Several of these poems appeared in the following anthologies: *Eyes Glowing at the Edge of the Woods: Fiction and Poetry from West Virginia* (Vandalia/WVU Press)—"Ritual," "Camping as Boys in the Cow Field"; *The Queer South: LGBTQ Writers on the American South* (Sibling Rivalry Press)—"Brave"; *Drawn to Marvel: Poems from the Comic Books* (Minor Arcana Press)—"Vampirella"; *A Constellation of Kisses* (Terrapin Books)—"Strawberries, Limoncello, Water Ice, Passing Time"; *The Best of Philadelphia Stories* (PS Books)—"Thirst"; *LGBTQ Fiction and Poetry from Appalachia* (WVU Press)—"Scrape the Velvet from Your Antlers," "Brave," "Vampirella," "Monkey Orchid," "Alien Boy," "Mercy," "Ritual."

In addition, a number of these poems appeared in the chapbook *Velvet Rodeo*, selected by poet C. Dale Young for the Bloom Prize, and in *Antlers*, a chapbook published as part of Seven Kitchens Press's Editors Series. My sincere thanks to Charles Flowers of Bloom Books and Ron Mohring of Seven Kitchens Press.

Grateful thanks is given to the Lambda Literary Writer's Retreat for Emerging LGBTQ Voices, the Sewanee Writers' Conference, Peter Murphy's Winter Poetry + Prose Getaway, and Millay Arts for support of this project. Thanks to C. Dale Young, Dorianne Laux, Reginald Dwayne Betts, and Brian Teare for selecting some of these poems for prizes along the way.

Thank you to Jeff Mann for graciously supplying an introduction.

Much thanks to J. Bruce Fuller, Karisma "Charlie" Tobin, PJ Carlisle, Bradley Alan Ivey, and the rest of the fine staff at Texas Review Press for bringing this book to life.

Eternal thanks to Dawn Manning for her generous help and insight. For friendship, inspiration, and help, my thanks goes out to Sonja Livingston, Shelley Puhak, Elaine Terranova, Valerie Fox, Jim Gladstone, Eduardo C. Corral, Tim Seibles, David Groff, Aaron Smith, Jonathan Corcoran, B. H. Fairchild, Sidney Wade, Sarah Rose Nordgren, George David Clark, Matt Miller, Jennifer Sperry Steinorth, Jeff Markovitz, Bill Lavender, Nancy Dixon, Jeni and Daniel Wallace, Steven Dunn, Bryan Borland, Dustin Brookshire, and Kazim Ali, headmaster of the 2015 Lambda Literary Retreat poetry cohort.

Last but not least, thank you to my parents and my family, and to John, who keeps the flame inside me burning.

About the Author

Kelly McQuain grew up in the Allegheny Mountains of West Virginia and is the author of two previous chapbooks, *Velvet Rodeo* (chosen by C. Dale Young for the Bloom Award) and *Antlers* (selected by Seven Kitchens Press for their Editor's Series). A Lambda Literary Fellow and a Sewanee Scholar, McQuain has published poetry in *Best New Poets 2000, American Poetry Review, The Pinch, Kestrel, Philadelphia Stories*, and *Appalachian Review*, as well as in numerous anthologies: *The Queer South: LGBTQ Writers on the American South, LGBTQ Fiction and Poetry from Appalachia*, and *Drawn to Marvel: Poems from the Comic Books*. Also an artist, McQuain has exhibited his paintings in books, journals, magazines, museums, and galleries. He currently works as a professor of English in Philadelphia.

www.KellyMcQuain.wordpress.com

CPSIA information can be obtained
at www.ICGtesting.com
Printed in the USA
JSHW021700170123
36202JS00002B/4